# PROGRAM GOALS

★ Teach students how to take ownership of their education.
★ Help teachers reach their goals with their students.
★ Include parents and other caregivers in this collaborative educational experience.

## MESSAGE to Teachers

The *Goal Setting for Students*™ program can be used to enhance any curriculum. This is not a stand alone program that takes valuable time out of your teaching day. Rather it gives your students the tools they need to understand how they play a significant role in *their* education. This program will assist you in reaching *your* goals with your students.

Education is a collaborative effort with you, the students and their parents/caregivers. This workbook gives your students instructions on what goals are and why they are important. *We bring the message "home" by teaching the students how they can use these techniques in YOUR class.*

The chapters include: *Defining Success, Principles of Goal Setting, Samples & Practice, Investing in Yourself, Measuring Your Progress, Meeting the Challenge, How to Get Started* and *Summary*. Each chapter is self-contained. The workbook has been divided into several sections within each chapter. This allows you to choose how to incorporate these important messages into your class activity.

The *Goal Setting for Students*™ will enhance your efforts and help you achieve *your* goals for the students. This program teaches students how to take ownership of *their* education and *their* future.

## MESSAGE to Parents and other Caregivers

The *Goal Setting for Students*™ program is a powerful tool for your child's future. The teachers will be showing the students how to set goals and how to make goal setting a habit for life. This is a joint effort with the student, the teachers and you to learn these valuable life lessons. We need your help to reinforce the classroom lessons.

We want the students to understand that they have some responsibility in their education. After completing the program we want them to ask themselves on a regular basis: "Am I putting forth my best effort in school?" This workbook in combination with the teacher and your efforts will help your student to answer "yes" to that question.

# Table Of

## Chapter 1: What is Success?
- Success means different things to different people.
- Success takes desire, planning, and action.

PAGE 8

## Chapter 6: Meeting the Challenges
- The value of determination.
- Four potential roadblocks to success.
- Eliminate excuses.

PAGE 48

## Chapter 7: How to Get Started

- Ten points to keep you focused.
- Where do you start.
- How to manage your time.

PAGE 56

## Chapter 5: Measuring Your Progress
- Two essential questions to ask each day.
- Taking responsibility.
- Why helping others is important.

PAGE 40

## Chapter 8: Summary
PAGE 62

# Contents

## Goal Setting

**CHAPTER 2** — PAGE 14
- Four strategic questions.
- Three key elements of goal setting.

## Samples & Practice

**CHAPTER 3** — PAGE 22
- The importance of "stretch" goals.
- Sample goals for school, personal, and sports/hobbies.
- How to develop a "YES! Count on Me" attitude.

## Investing In Yourself

**CHAPTER 4** — PAGE 32
- The importance of being positive.
- How to improve your self-image.
- "Bummer words" that hold you back.

# CHAPTER 1

# Introduction: What is SUCCESS?

## What To Expect
★ Learn that *Success* means different things to people.
★ *Success* takes planning.
★ *Success* takes time.
★ *Success* takes action.

### Words to Remember
- Accomplishment
- *Success*
- Desire
- Commitment

## Preview

THE word *success* means many things to many people. For example, Hector may think *success* is helping others by developing a new medicine to cure a disease. Laura might define *success* as being a star athlete, while Kisha thinks getting good grades in school is a measure of *success*. To Roz being a teacher is how she will define *success*. Hector, Laura, Kisha and Roz are all correct. *Success* is all of these things and more.

RALPH WALDO EMERSON defined success as: "To laugh often and much; to win the respect of intelligent people and the affection of children; ... to appreciate beauty, to find the best in others; to leave the world a little better; whether by a healthy child or a garden patch ... to know even one life has breathed easier because you have lived. This is success." Contributing to the happiness and success of others is an important component of your own success.

IN this manual you will discuss what success means to you and how goal setting can help you reach your full potential. You will learn how to set and achieve goals, how to measure your progress toward reaching them, how to invest in yourself and the importance of helping others. You will learn about taking responsibility, how to overcome roadblocks to success and you will find the "Bummer Words" that hold you back from reaching your full potential. You will also learn how to incorporate these lessons in the classroom and in your everyday life.

THE dictionary defines *success* as "accomplishing or completing a desire or want." It lies in your ability to want something bad enough (a goal) that you are willing to put in extra effort to reach it. *Success* is not walking through life hoping something good happens to you. Your *success* begins by making decisions about what you want and about what is important to you. These decisions become your goals. Once you have set your mind on a goal, then write it down, create an *Action Plan* and make it happen. (This manual, and the discussions you will have, will help you in this process).

THERE are goals that you set on a daily basis that might include making sure you hand in your homework on time and that you take the time to check to make sure it is correct. Goals may be medium range in length. An example of this might be to bring your science grade up one letter by the next report card which is six weeks away. You will learn that goals may be large and take a long time to complete. One example of a long-term goal may be to go to college.

GOALS may be big or small; they can be about school, home, personal, sports or many other things. All goals have two things in common — *desire and action*. First, you have to <u>really</u>, <u>really</u> want your goals to become a reality and you have to take action toward reaching your goal.

YOU will find that being *success*ful can become a habit, but it will take effort on your part. This is a key point — by learning and doing what is described in this manual, you can develop a pattern, or habit, for success. When you make goal setting a habit in your life it can lead you to your success. <u>Success</u> takes time. <u>Success</u> takes desire. <u>Success</u> takes action. <u>Success</u> takes commitment. *Commitment* is a promise you make to yourself to keep working to reach your goal even if the going gets tough.

IN the next several sessions we will talk about what a goal is, how to set and accomplish goals and how to check your progress toward reaching your goals.

THIS manual includes several sample goals for you to review, and a section on how to get started. You will discover that there can be potential roadblocks to your *success*. We will help you identify them and avoid them because we want you to be *success*ful. This manual is about you and **FOR YOU**. However you define *success*, this manual will give you the tools to reach your goals.

Let's review the important components of success:
1. *Success* means different things to different people.
2. *Success* is setting goals and accomplishing them.
3. *Success* takes planning and a strong desire.
4. *Success* is taking action.
5. *Success* means reaching your goals even when the going gets tough.

# Key Vocabulary Words

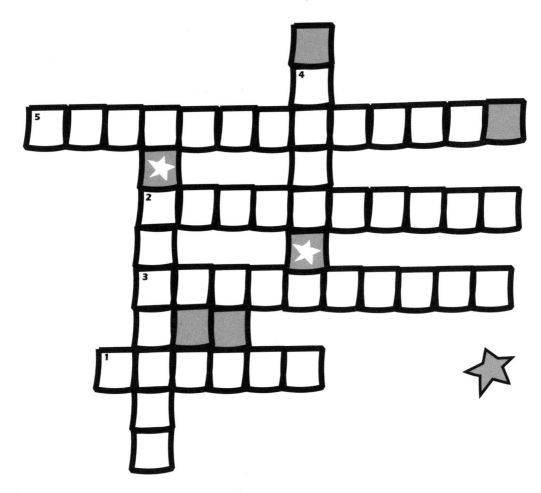

**Fill in the blanks with one of the words from the list below.**

*Desire*          *Accomplished*
*Time*            *Success*
*Successful*      *Commitment*

## ACROSS

1. All goals have two things in common - _____ and action.

2. I want to be _____, and I am willing to plan and put in the effort and time.

3. A promise is a _____ to do something for yourself or others.

5. When I have _____ my goal, it means I have reached it.

## DOWN

2. _____ is setting goals and accomplishing them.

4. *Success* does not happen overnight, it takes _____.

**Goal Setting for Students**

**Class Activity**

**1.** How would you define success in this class? Is it getting a certain grade, handing in your homework on time, listening better in class or are there other ways you would define success for this class? Explain.

**2.** Re-read the quote from Ralph Waldo Emerson in the "Preview" section of this chapter. How is this definition of success different from the images you see in magazines and on TV? Explain.

**3.** What does success mean to you?

**4.** "The secret to success is to do the common thing uncommonly well."

*Anonymous*

Do you agree with this quote? Why or why not?

**5.** Name three people you think are *success*ful and why?

**Name**        **Why**

1. _____  _____
2. _____  _____
3. _____  _____

## Home Activity

**1.** What two things did you learn about *success* from this lesson?

1. _____
2. _____

**2.** Ask your parents/caregivers to name three people they consider to be *successful* and why.

| Name | Why |
|------|-----|
|      |     |
|      |     |
|      |     |

**3.** Below is a list of things you can do to become more *success*ful in class.

Choose two actions that you will accomplish in the next week to help you succeed in class.

### *How can I be more successful in class?*

- ☐ Listen better in class.
- ☐ Learn how to take better classroom notes.
- ☐ Take part in the classroom discussions.
- ☐ Look over the chapter *before* it is discussed in class.
- ☐ Read the chapter and review my class notes before doing my homework.
- ☐ Ask the teacher questions if I did not understand the material.
- ☐ Make sure I write down the homework assignments correctly.
- ☐ Three days before a test, spend *extra* time studying.
- ☐ The night before the test ask someone to help me study.
- ☐ Do a project for extra credit.
- ☐ Change my seating assignment in class.
- ☐ Hand in my homework on time.
- ☐ Take a few moments to check my homework *before* handing it in.
- ☐ Ask a classmate for help.

**4.** Find two pictures in magazines of people you define as successful. One of the pictures should be of a male and the other a female. On a separate sheet of paper write a paragraph for each picture about why you feel they are successful. (Note: In your paragraphs answer this question: Why do you think goals were important to the people in your pictures?)

**5.** "Be honest and work hard to get what you want. Don't take shortcuts; you are only cheating yourself in the long run. Success is not measured by money or fame, but by how you fell about your own goals and accomplishments and the time and effort you put into them."   ***Willie Stargell***

Discuss with your parents/ caregivers what this quote means to you.

# Chapter 2: Goal Setting

## What To Expect

★ What are goals?

★ The difference between a goal and a dream.

★ Why are goals important?

★ How do you set a goal?

## Words to Remember

Day Dreams
Goal Setting
Action Steps
Target Date

## Preview

IN the next two chapters we will discuss goal setting and how to use goals in your classroom and in your everyday life. This chapter will give you the basics while the next chapter will give you additional information and some sample goals and practice.

THERE are many things that young people and adults think about during their day that they would like. These dreams, or wishes, can range from wanting a hamburger after school, to wanting to go on a summer vacation, or thinking about what you want to be when you grow up. This wishful thinking is often referred to as *daydreaming*. Everyone has daydreams and spends part of their day daydreaming.

MOST people have several daydreams during the day. Some are just simply fun to think about, but you don't have any control over them. You might daydream about having your school's basketball team win their game on Wednesday, but if you are not the coach or one of the players, you won't have much control over the outcome of the game. But it is still fun to daydream about the exciting basketball game on Wednesday.

THERE are also many daydreams or wishes that you do have the power to control. Yes, you do! You can do something to make those daydreams come true. That's the good news. However, you _will_ have to do more than simply close your eyes and hold your breath until the dream comes true.

GOAL Setting is the key to making your dreams come true. *Goal Setting* is thinking about something that you want, writing it down on paper, developing a plan to make it happen and setting a date to complete the goal. *Goal Setting* is like shooting an arrow toward a target. You may want to hit the target, but if you don't take action—shooting the arrow toward the target—you will only have a dream. The difference between a dream and a goal is action.

FOUR key Goal Setting questions that will keep you focused on what is important to your continued success. The BIG FOUR are:

THE first two questions will give you information about the goal - what it is and why it is important to you. Your answers to these questions will help you to define the goal. Question #3 is about setting in motion a plan – Action Steps to achieve your goal. The last question gives you a target date for completion.

ACTION STEPS help you to move toward the goal. They help you to get started and they move you closer to completing your goal. *Action Steps* are like steps on a ladder and the top rung is your goal. As you accomplish each of the *Action Steps* you are getting closer to completing your goal.

IN Goal Setting you will want to set Target Dates for completion. A target date can be a day, a week, a month, your next exam or the next soccer practice, etc. It is important to create a reasonable time frame of when you will complete your goal.

BE realistic with the goals that you establish. Set yourself up for *success*. If you set a goal to be an NBA basketball player and no one in your family is over 5'4", you may want to review your goal. If everyone in the NBA is one to two feet taller than you, then your goal may not be realistic. Your goals should broaden your capabilities and when achieved give you satisfaction and a sense of accomplishment. Set realistic goals and grow.

## 1. Challenge
**WHY DO I WANT IT?**
Define the desire or challenge facing you.

## 2. Goal
**WHAT DO I WANT?**
Write down the goal you want to achieve.

## 3. Action Steps
**HOW WILL I GET IT?**
Your specific action plan to reach your goal.

## 4. Target Dates
**WHEN DO I WANT IT?**
The completion date to reach your goal.

Let's review the three important components of goal setting:

**1.** Turn your dreams into goals by <u>writing them on paper</u>.

**2.** Write down *Action Steps* you need to complete to reach your goal. Remember to think of them as the steps of a ladder and the goal is the top of that ladder. Each Action Step you complete moves you closer to the top of the ladder or your goal.

**3.** Set a <u>Target Dates</u> for completion of your goal.

**4.** The four key Goals Setting questions you need to ask yourself are:

    a). Why do I want it?    c). How will I get it?

    b). What do I want?    d). When do I want it?

## Key Vocabulary Words

**1.** Fill in the missing words in each sentence with the correct word below.

| *Goals* | *Successful* | *Write* |
|---|---|---|
| *Action Steps* | *Goal Setting* | *Daydreams* |
| *Target Date* | *Action* | |

1. It is important to _____ down your goals.

2. *Success*ful people have _____.

3. The difference between a dream and a goal is _____.

4. In goal setting it is important to have a _____ for completion.

5. Everyone has _____.

6. _____ are like steps on a ladder.

7. I want to be a _____ person.

8. Learning about _____ is an important part of growing up.

Tyronne was an average student who worked hard for his grades. He received his report card and was disappointed that his science grade was not higher. Tyronne knew that if he wanted to get a higher grade, it was going to take extra effort on his part. He knew it was his responsibility.

At home he decided to turn his wish into a goal. First, he wrote down on a piece of paper the higher grade he wanted for the science course. Next, he wrote down the *Action Steps*, or ladder rungs, he needed to complete in order to reach his goal of a higher grade in science.

The *Action Steps* Tyronne wrote included:

1. Talking to the teacher to find out what he could do for extra credit.
2. Study an extra 15 minutes each night on science.
3. Asking his parents to give him oral quizzes on what he learned from the homework.
4. Study hard the night before a test, get a good night's rest and try not to worry about the science test.

The last item Tyronne wrote on the paper was the date when he planned to complete the goal. Then, as a daily reminder, he put the paper with his goal and plan on the desk where he did his homework. Each time he finished an Action Step, he checked it off the paper. When the next reporting period ended, Tyronne had accomplished his goal of receiving a higher grade in science.

## DREAM + ACTION STEPS + TARGET DATES = GOAL

This is *your* life, *your* goals and *your* success.
You are a ***Winner!***

1. Below is a list of activities students do during the course of a month. In the right hand column are the words Always, Sometimes, Not Very Often and Never. Indicate how often you do these activities **without being asked**.

|  | Always | Sometimes | Not Often | Never |
|---|---|---|---|---|
| Clean my room |  |  |  |  |
| Do my homework |  |  |  |  |
| Help in the kitchen |  |  |  |  |
| Read a book |  |  |  |  |
| Exercise |  |  |  |  |
| Volunteer to help a neighbor |  |  |  |  |
| Take out the trash |  |  |  |  |
| Read a magazine |  |  |  |  |
| Mow the lawn |  |  |  |  |
| Watch TV |  |  |  |  |
| Play with my friends |  |  |  |  |
| Extra credit project at school |  |  |  |  |
| Iron my clothes |  |  |  |  |
| Wash the family car |  |  |  |  |
| Go to the library to study |  |  |  |  |

2. Goal Setting Example # 1:

Look at the list above again and circle the one area that you want to improve during the next week. Let's see how you can change your desire to improve into a goal with Action Steps and a target date. Please write your goal (the item you circled) below.

**My goal for the next week is:** _____

The ACTION STEPS that I need to complete in order to reach my goal are:

1. _____
2. _____
3. _____

My Target Date to complete my goal is: _____.

**3.** Goal Setting Example # 2

Think about this class. Let's see how you can bring your grade up on the next test. Below list your goal, your Action Steps for completing the goal and a target date for completion.

The subject I want to improve in is: _____.

My grade on the last test was _____.

My **Goal** is to bring my _____ grade up to a _____.
    (subject)                                      (grade)

Some examples of Action Steps needed to be completed in order to achieve the higher grade may be: doing extra homework, spending 15 minutes a night studying that subject, asking more questions in class, listening better, etc. Which **ACTION STEPS** will you take to reach your goal?

The **ACTION STEPS** that I need to complete in order to reach my goal are:

1. _____
2. _____
3. _____
4. _____

My **Target Date** to complete my goal is: _____

**4.** "Set goals for yourself and work hard to achieve them. Some goals you will achieve and others you won't, but at least you will have the satisfaction of knowing where you are."   ***Beth Daniel***

Do you agree with this quote? Explain.

_____
_____
_____

# Home Activity

**1.** Find a quote that inspires you to do your best. You may find it in a book, a magazine, or it may be a favorite saying your teacher has. Write it down in your notebook and highlight it so you can see it everyday.

**2.** What are the three things you need to make a goal?

1. _____
2. _____
3. _____

**3.** Why is it important to write your goals down on paper?

_____
_____
_____
_____

**4.** With your parents decide on a goal that you can complete during the next week. Have them help you list the Action Steps and decide on a completion date.

**My GOAL for this week is:** _____

**ACTION STEPS** that you and your parents/caregivers develop together.

1. _____
2. _____
3. _____

The **TARGET DATE** to complete my goal is: _____

**5.** Discuss with your parents/caregivers what this quote means to you.

*"What is worth doing is worth doing well."*

# CHAPTER 3 — Samples & Practice

## What To Expect
★ Define the challenge correctly
★ Sample goals for personal, sports/hobbies, school

**Words to Remember**
Challenge
Stretch goals
"I'LL MAKE IT HAPPEN"
Attitude

## Preview

IN the previous chapter, we learned about Goals, Action Steps and the importance of setting a Target Date for completing your goals. This session will give you some "hands on" experience on how to set goals and establish specific Action Steps. But first, let's add a couple of more thoughts about goals:

1. Define the challenge.
2. "Stretch goals" and why they are important.
3. The power of an *"YES! Count On Me"* attitude.

★ **DEFINE THE CHALLENGE:** It is important to clearly define the challenge you are trying to overcome. Let's say you are in an archery contest. The good news is you shot an arrow into the middle of the target- the bull's-eye and you should receive 10 points toward the archery championship. The bad news is you hit the wrong target and you won't receive the points. Goal setting is very similar. You have to make sure you are setting your goals for the correct challenge or target.

**EXAMPLE #1:** You are not getting the grade in English that you think you deserve. You define the challenge as "the English teacher just doesn't like me" so you don't try very hard in that class.

22  Goal Setting for Students

**QUESTION:**

What would you do differently if you defined the challenge as "not enough effort on my part"?

**THAT** is a different "**TARGET**." If that was the case, rather than not trying very hard, you would have set a goal and a plan of action to increase your effort in the English class so you could get the higher grade.

**EXAMPLE #2:** You have a part-time job after school, but you are not making as much money as you think you should. You think the pay is not worth the effort so you decide to quit and spend more time with your friends.

**QUESTION:**

Will you talk to your boss before you quit?

**BY** getting a better view of what the challenge might be, you have the potential of a much different outcome. In this case, you have a meeting with your boss to talk about a raise. In that meeting you might ask "How am I doing?" and "How can I can earn some extra money?" After that conversation, you might look at that part-time job in a completely different way. Also, you may have found a way to earn additional money.

**MAKE** certain that you clearly and correctly define the challenge.

**★ STRETCH GOALS:** Goal setting helps you accomplish more. If your goals are too easy then you may not reach your potential. It is important to set goals that "**STRETCH**" and extend your abilities. Make sure the goals you set are achievable and that you have to give some extra effort to complete.

**A** cautionary note: There is a difference between a stretch goal and an unrealistic goal. Let's explore. Your room is messy so you set a goal to make your bed everyday. You know that this is a pretty easy goal to accomplish, and that it won't take much effort on your part. A "stretch goal" might be to have a fairly clean room before you go to school. This might include making the bed, closing the closet door and picking up the dirty clothes on the floor. This may be a "stretch" goal for you, but is it realistic?

**AN** unrealistic goal, considering how messy your room currently is, would be to have your room sparkling clean before you go to school each day. Sparkling clean might include vacuuming and dusting in addition to the above activities for the "stretch" goal. You may find this to be unrealistic at this time.

**EACH** of us need goals that stretch our abilities. Make sure that with some effort on your part - **STRETCH** - you can accomplish your goal. Set your goals for success! Then, build on those successes!

**★"YES! COUNT ON ME" attitude:** In the sample goals in this chapter you will see that all of the sentences are in a positive "YES! Count On Me" format. Words like "I can" and "I will" should be in all of your written goals and Action Steps. By writing them this way, your goals and Action Steps are expressed in an up-beat and positive way. Mary Kay Ash who built an international cosmetics company said: "If you think you can – you can." Reaching your goals will give you an "YES! Count On Me" attitude. Remember to write your goals down and put action to your Action Steps. Also, you will find it valuable to read your goals for each day – better yet, say them out loud to yourself. By doing this, you will be reminded on a daily basis what your goals are, and you can review how you are doing with completing your Action Steps.

## REAL World Example

Below are several examples of goals that you might have for school, personal and sports/hobbies. You will notice that in each section we have a couple of fully competed goals. Also, we have a couple of goals that require you to finish the Action Steps and the Target Date. In the last section - "Now It's Your Turn" - we ask you to define your challenge, write your goal down and develop your own Action Steps and target date.

### SCHOOL

| | |
|---|---|
| **CHALLENGE** | I am capable of doing better in my classroom activities. |
| **GOAL** | I will put more effort into each class. |
| **ACTION STEPS** | 1. I will listen better and take more notes in class.<br>2. I will ask the teacher if I can do something for extra credit.<br>3. I will take 10 minutes the night before class to look over the subject material.<br>4. I will participate more in classroom discussions. |
| **TARGET DATE** | Starting today |

© John Bishop 2003

### SCHOOL

| | |
|---|---|
| **CHALLENGE** | I get really nervous before a test. |
| **GOAL** | I will stay calm before and during my tests. |
| **ACTION STEPS** | 1. I will do my homework each night and check to make sure it is correct.<br>2. I will take a few minutes each night to review what we studied during school that day.<br>3. If I know I have a test coming in a couple of days, I will study that subject an extra 15 minutes each night.<br>5. I will get good night's rest before my test.<br>6. Just before I begin the exam, I will say to myself: "I studied hard, I am a good student, I am prepared, and I will do well." |
| **TARGET DATE** | Next 30 days |

© John Bishop 2003

**1.** In the next sample, complete the Action Steps and the Target Date to accomplish the goal.

## SCHOOL

| CHALLENGE | I have not been handing my homework in "on time." |
|---|---|
| GOAL | I will hand all homework assignments in on time for the next two weeks. |
| ACTION STEPS | 1. I will make sure I get the assignments and that I understand what is expected of me.<br><br>2. _____<br><br>3. _____<br><br>4. _____ |
| TARGET DATE | For the next two weeks starting today |

© John Bishop 2003

## SCHOOL

| CHALLENGE | I know it is important to participate in class, but I'm afraid I'll make a mistake. |
|---|---|
| GOAL | I will conquer my fear of making a mistake in class discussions. |
| Action Steps | 1. I will listen better in class.<br><br>2. I will make sure I have done my homework on time.<br><br>3. _____<br><br>4. _____ |
| TARGET DATE | |

© John Bishop 2003

Samples & Practice

# PERSONAL

| CHALLENGE | I need to improve my reading skills. |
|---|---|
| GOAL | I will read a book each month that is not required by my teachers. |
| ACTION STEPS | 1. I will go to the library each week.<br>2. I will find magazines on subjects that interest me.<br>3. I will find 30 minutes each day to read about a subject that I want to learn more about.<br>4. I will turn off the TV and not take phone calls from friends between 7:00 and 8:30 each night. |
| TARGET DATE | Now |

© John Bishop 2003

# PERSONAL

| CHALLENGE | People always seem to be nagging me. |
|---|---|
| GOAL | I want to do things before I have to be told ("nagged"). |
| ACTION STEPS | 1. I will write down the chores I am responsible for at home and I will do them before being asked.<br>2. I will do one additional chore not on my list because I want to help someone else.<br>3. I will volunteer to help a neighbor or friend.<br>4. I realize that it is my responsibility to do well in school, and I will continue to do well in my studies. |
| TARGET DATE | Immediately |

© John Bishop 2003

**Goal Setting for Students**

## PERSONAL

| CHALLENGE | I don't seem to "fit in" at school. |
|---|---|
| GOAL | I want people to like me for the person I am – not for the person they want me to be. |
| ACTION STEPS | 1. Each morning before school, I will say "I am a good person and if a few kids at school don't see that, then they aren't seeing what I have to offer - the real me."<br>2. I will ask for help from students, parents, counselors or teachers.<br>3. I will join one of the school clubs or sports teams.<br>4. I will help others by volunteering at school or in activities after school.<br>5. I will lead others instead of following them. |
| TARGET DATE | Start today |

© John Bishop 2003

**2.** In the next sample goal complete the Action Steps and the Target Date you think are needed to accomplish the goal.

## PERSONAL

| CHALLENGE | There is a lot of peer pressure from other kids to start smoking. |
|---|---|
| GOAL | I know smoking is not good for me and that it is expensive. I will not smoke. |
| Action Steps | 1. I will start to exercise more.<br>2. I will leave when people try to get me to smoke.<br>3. _____<br>4. _____ |
| Target Date | |

© John Bishop 2003

Samples & Practice

## SPORTS & HOBBIES

| CHALLENGE | I like soccer, but I'm not as good as some of my teammates. |
|---|---|
| GOAL | *I will make a solid improvement in my soccer abilities this year.* |
| ACTION STEPS | 1. I will spend an extra 15 minutes each day on kicking and passing drills – even on days when there is no practice.<br>2. I will work on using both feet equally well for passing and kicking.<br>3. I will practice with someone who is more experienced than me so that I can learn from them.<br>4. I will read books about soccer and will watch soccer matches on TV to learn from the very best.<br>5. After the season is over, I will continue to practice so that I can improve for next year. |
| TARGET DATE | All season |

© John Bishop 2003

## SPORTS & HOBBIES

| CHALLENGE | I want to earn a Black Belt in Karate. |
|---|---|
| GOAL | *I will practice and study to get my Black Belt.* |
| ACTION STEPS | 1. I will get to class 15 minutes early.<br>2. I will listen to the instructor and practice hard in class each day.<br>3. I will work out with the students with the higher belts to learn from them.<br>4. I will ask for help when I am unsure of a technique.<br>5. At home I will practice 30 minutes/day on my forms, kicking, punches and blocks.<br>6. I will enter the karate tournaments to gain more experience and confidence. |
| Target Date | Start immediately. |

© John Bishop 2003

**2.** In the next two sample goals, complete the Action Steps and target date you think are needed to accomplish the goal.

## SPORTS & HOBBIES

| CHALLENGE | Cooking has always interested me. |
|---|---|
| GOAL | *I will learn to cook well.* |
| ACTION STEPS | 1. _____<br>2. _____<br>3. _____<br>4. _____ |
| TARGET DATE | |

© John Bishop 2003

## SPORTS & HOBBIES

| CHALLENGE | I want to learn how to draw. |
|---|---|
| GOAL | *I will enter a drawing contest at the end of the semester.* |
| ACTION STEPS | 1. _____<br>2. _____<br>3. _____<br>4. _____ |
| TARGET DATE | |

© John Bishop 2003

Samples & Practice

Let's review:

1. Remember to <u>clearly define your challenge.</u>
2. Use "<u>I can</u>" and "<u>I will</u>" wording for your goal and Action Steps.
3. <u>Read your goals everyday.</u>
4. Make them realistic but "<u>stretch" your abilities</u>.
5. You are a ***Winner***!

## Now It's Your Turn

Below are three blank sections to use for your goals. Challenge yourself with a goal for School, Sport/Hobby, and Personal.

### SCHOOL

| CHALLENGE | |
|---|---|
| GOAL | |
| ACTION STEPS | 1. _____ <br> 2. _____ <br> 3. _____ <br> 4. _____ |
| TARGET DATE | |

© John Bishop 2003

## SPORTS & HOBBIES

| CHALLENGE | |
|---|---|
| GOAL | |
| ACTION STEPS | 1. <br> 2. <br> 3. <br> 4. |
| TARGET DATE | |

© John Bishop 2003

## PERSONAL

| CHALLENGE | |
|---|---|
| GOAL | |
| ACTION STEPS | 1. <br> 2. <br> 3. <br> 4. |
| TARGET DATE | |

© John Bishop 2003

Samples & Practice

# CHAPTER 4: Invest In Yourself

**What To Expect**
- ★ How to improve your self image.
- ★ Words that hold you back from reaching your goals.
- ★ The importance of being positive.

**Words to Remember**
- "I'll Make It Happen" Words
- Bummer Words
- Mentor
- Inner voice

## Preview

*"Life is not about finding yourself. Life is about creating yourself."*
George Bernard Shaw

AS a young person growing up, you are learning about yourself. You are finding out what you like and what you don't, what you are good at and what takes extra effort on your part. You are on a journey to learn about yourself and your surrounding. Importantly, you have an opportunity to "create yourself."

YOU "create yourself" by developing an "YES! Count On Me" attitude. This comes from your accomplishments for yourself and for others. This chapter is all about attitude. You play an essential role in the development of an "YES! Count On Me" attitude. Here are five major ways to invest in yourself and develop an "YES! Count On Me" attitude:

1. Use your inner voice to your advantage.
2. Use the "YES! Count On Me" words.
3. Minimize the "Bummer Words."
4. Have a positive self-image.
5. Spend time with a mentor.

32  Goal Setting for Students

**INNER VOICE:** What in the world is an inner voice, and how can you use it to your advantage? Everybody talks to themselves. Yes, everyone! Your inner voice speaks to you several times during a day. Some will think that is their parent's way of talking to them "long distance." Others will think it is a voice from within to help them navigate through the day's activities. A few might think the inner voice is coming from mean Aunt Martha who never liked them.

**HOWEVER** you think of the inner voice, everyone has one. It might remind you to do something or it might give you a great idea. Your inner voice might tell you to watch out for cars when crossing the street or it might remind you to be careful when doing something new. There is one important thing to remember about your inner voice–you control the on/off switch. Nobody else but you can control your inner voice.

**NOW** here is where it gets interesting. If you are at the controls of your inner voice, will you let in positive thoughts or negative thoughts? Has your inner voice ever said to you: "I can't do that," "I'm not good at this" or "I'll never be able to do that?" These are all negative messages your inner voice is giving you. Since you are in control of your inner voice, why not create positive messages? Turn your inner voice to your advantage.

**YES! COUNT ON ME words:** Use positive "YES! Count On Me" words: **YES, I WILL** and **I CAN**. Remember, everyone talks to themselves. You are at the controls of your inner voice. You can let in either negative or positive messages. Choose positive upbeat words for a more successful life. These words will help you to develop an "YES! Count On Me" attitude. You are a winner! Tell yourself that you are a winner everyday with "yes, I will and I can" messages.

**BUMMER WORDS:** It is equally important to minimize the "*Bummer Words.*" These words are the opposite of the "YES! Count On Me" words. Bummer words hold you back from reaching your full potential. They are negative and can often stop you before you even get started. For example, "I'll never get a good grade on that test," or "I'll try it, but I won't be any good," or "If only I was taller."

**THE six Bummer Words are:** no, never, can't, won't, if and maybe. Many people use these words as an excuse. One of your goals should be to minimize the number of times in a day that you use the Bummer Words.

**IF** you are serious about goal setting and being successful, then you have to be serious about minimizing excuses and negative words. Count the number of times in a day you use the **BUMMER WORDS:** no, never, can't, won't, if, and maybe. Now, replace them with the positive "YES! Count On Me" words: can, will and yes. For example, "I will do that for you," or "I can get a better grade," or "Yes, I will do my homework".

**SELF-IMAGE:** This is how you see yourself. Your self-image can be positive or negative. It is your choice. Earlier we learned about the importance of having positive inner voice messages. Your inner voice is a great contributor to your self-image. Having a positive self-image (how you see yourself) and using positive inner voice messages (what your inner voice says to you) are excellent ways to invest in yourself.

**DO** you think you would have a positive self-image if your inner voice messages included: "I'm doing well" or "I helped that lady today, and that feels good; I'm a good person" or "the big exam is today, I've studied hard, I'm ready and I'm going to do well." **It is important for you to believe in yourself and in your abilities. You should greet each new day with a smile and an "YES! COUNT ON ME" attitude.**

**MENTOR:** A mentor is another way to invest in yourself. You might think of a mentor as a coach or a personal advisor. It may be easier to explain this concept by using an example we are all familiar with. Often we look at a successful coach and see how that person has guided young men or women to reach new heights. This is what a mentor can do for you.

A mentor doesn't have to be a sports coach, but you want to find someone who can help you reach new heights. A mentor is a person who can help you look at problems and opportunities from a different point of view and someone who can teach you from their life experiences. A mentor should be someone you trust. A mentor can give you advice on ways to do things correctly and things to look out for that may cause you problems. Importantly, the mentor can guide you to making the right choices.

**Let's review the important components of investing in yourself.**

1. You <u>control the on/off switch</u> for your inner voice.
2. Invest in yourself with "<u>YES! Count On Me</u>" words: I can, I will and yes.
3. Minimize the Bummer Words.
4. Find a <u>mentor</u> to be a personal coach and advisor.
5. Greet each day with a smile and say "I am a WINNER! I am successful."

## Key Vocabulary Words

Fill in the blanks with one of the words from the list below.

| Invest | Mentor | "YES! Count On Me" words |
| Inner voice | Bummer words | |

1. Everyday I will use the _____ like yes, I can and I will.
2. I am at the controls of my _____.
3. It is important to _____ in myself with a positive self-image.
4. I will minimize the _____: if, can't, won't, maybe, never and no.
5. A_____ can be my personal advisor.

**34** Goal Setting for Students

### Real World Example

Pete loved to play on the school basketball team. Pete was not as tall as some of the other kids, but he really wanted to be a good player. He invested in himself by working extra hard at practice. When he was shooting baskets his inner voice would give him positive messages that he was a good player. On weekends, he was always playing pick up games with his older brothers.

Sometimes when Pete could not find someone to play basketball with, he would shoot baskets alone for long periods. When he did this, Pete would pretend that he was playing on a team for the state championship. He imagined he was the person the team relied for the game winning shot with time running out.

On the last game of the season, Pete got to live his dream. There were 10 seconds on the clock and Pete had the ball. The fans were on their feet yelling. He was about to take the game-winning shot.

Do you think he went to the bench and said, "Coach, I'm afraid? You should have someone else take the shot?" Or, do you think he went over to the PA system and said "I have not been working very hard at practice this week so don't expect me to make this shot?"

He knew he was ready to take the last shot. He worked hard at practice, listened to his coach and used positive messages to reassure himself that he was ready. Pete had earned the right to take the game winning shot. Whether he makes the shot or not, he has already won because he has invested in himself.

You may not be the basketball player in this story, but you have new situations everyday taking tests, meeting new people, doing chores at home, helping a friend or learning something new in class. Are you ready? Have you invested in yourself?

Invest in Yourself

## Class Activity

**1.** What three ways did Pete invest in himself in order to be prepared for the game winning shot?

**2.** If Pete does not make the last-minute shot how should he feel?

**3.** Whether it is practicing basketball, going to piano lessons or doing your homework to the best of your ability, you will have to invest time and energy. This is time you may have used for "hanging" with your friends, listening to music, watching TV, or playing video games. Why is it important to take time to invest in yourself?

**4.** "Goals determine your thoughts. Thoughts determine your life."

*Anonymous*

What does this quote mean to you? Explain.

**5.** Some students wonder why they have to learn a particular subject. They say " I'll never use this so why learn it." Each subject is important - whether it's math, science, visual arts, language, world cultures, health, physical education, etc. If you look around you will see many ways the "I'll never need it" subject can be helpful to you in everyday life. Write 10 examples of how you can use one of the subjects mentioned above in you life.

Examples of how _____ can be useful in my everyday life.
(subject)

1. _____  2. _____
3. _____  4. _____
5. _____  6. _____
7. _____  8. _____
9. _____  10. _____

**6.** There are reasons why a person may have a negative self-image. These students may still want to "fit in" but have trouble doing so. If you have a friend with a low self-image, how would you help them to feel more positive about themselves?

_____
_____
_____

Home Activity

**1.** In this chapter, we discussed that a *mentor* is a person who can guide you as you grow and learn. A mentor is someone you respect and trust, and a person who will give you good advice. A mentor can be a teacher, a parent, a relative, a neighbor or a coach. Ask your parents to name two people who have been mentors or coaches for them. How have their mentors helped them?

1. _____
2. _____

Invest in Yourself

**2.** Now it's your turn. Name one person in your life who has been a mentor or coach to you. How has your mentor helped you?

_____
_____
_____

**3.** Positive inner voice words include: Yes, I can and I will. Do you use these words often?     Yes _____     No _____

**4.** Today your inner voice may have spoken to you several times. It might have been in class, on the schoolyard, on the bus or at home. Was your inner voice positive?     Yes _____     No _____

**5.** How often do you use the Bummer Words (never, if, maybe, no, can't, won't) during the day?

        1 - 3 times per day?     _____

        4 – 7 times per day?     _____

        8 + times per day?     _____

**6.** "Success comes in cans, not in can nots."

*John Ralston*

Discuss with your parents/caregivers what this quote means to you.

_____
_____
_____

7. Set a goal to use less Bummer Words during the day. Below are examples of Action Steps, but this is your goal so add your Action Steps and your Target Date.

## BUMMER WORDS

| CHALLENGE | I use the Bummer Words - never, if, maybe, no, can't, won't - more than I want during my day. |
|---|---|
| GOAL | I will use fewer Bummer Words. |
| ACTION STEPS | 1. Today, I will count the number of times I say a Bummer Word. Tomorrow I will use one less Bummer Word.<br>2. I will not use Bummer Words in school.<br>3. I will put a rubber band on my wrist and snap it each time I use a Bummer Word.<br>4. _____<br>5. _____ |
| TARGET DATE | |

© John Bishop 2003

8. Below is a list of ways you can invest in yourself. You will note that some of the items are directed toward you and others are ways that you can help someone else. Circle one activity you will do in the next week to invest in yourself.

| | |
|---|---|
| Read a book | Help my brother/sister |
| Write in a daily journal | Keep my room clean |
| Use "I will" and "I can" words | Read a magazine |
| Study an extra 15 minutes each day | Help make dinner |
| Wash the family car | Listen better in class |
| Write my goals down each day | Learn from my mistakes |
| Do something for others | Write a letter to a relative |
| Eliminate "can't" from my day | Exercise |
| Try something that is different | Hand my homework in on time |

Invest in Yourself

# CHAPTER 5: Measure Your Progress

## What To Expect
★ Two important questions to ask yourself everyday.
★ Why helping others is important.
★ How to measure your progress toward reaching your goals.

**Words to Remember**
- Reality time
- Responsibility

## Preview

SO far, we have learned that there are many definitions for *success*. We have discussed how to set a goal, what Action Steps are and the importance of setting a target date for completing your goal(s). Also, we have learned about the importance of *"investing in yourself"* with positive messages.

AS you begin to use goal setting as a valuable tool in your life, it is important to check your progress toward reaching your goals. There are five ways to measure your progress:

1. Reality time
2. Checking your self-image
3. Taking responsibility
4. Completing your specific Action Steps
5. Helping others

**REALITY TIME:** Reality time is a time to "look at yourself in a mirror." It is an opportunity for you to look at how you are doing in reaching your goals. It is a time during each day when you take a couple of minutes for yourself - a time to reflect on how your day is going. You can do this by finding a quiet spot where you are alone - yes, alone.

TAKE a couple of minutes to stop the day's

40  **Goal Setting for Students**

activities and answer two reality time

QUESTIONS:

1. Am I giving my best effort to today's activities?
2. Am I making progress toward reaching my goal(s)?

IT is important to be honest. Sure, you can make excuses or blame others for not reaching your goal. Yes, you can be dishonest about your effort toward reaching your goal. But, why? You will be cheating yourself. This is your life, your goals and your success. Take a few moments each day to give an honest review of your efforts. Make it a habit to ask these questions about your effort everyday. You will find they are important to your success.

CHECKING Your Self-Image: In the last chapter we discussed the importance of "investing in yourself" with positive messages. To reach your goals, it is very important to have a positive mental attitude. One good way to check your progress toward reaching your goals is by checking your attitude. Do you have a positive attitude? Are you using more of the positive "I'll Make It Happen" words and less of the **BUMMER** words that can hold you back?

LET'S say that you set a goal to get a "B" on a project. You were given two weeks to complete the project, but now with three days left you have barely gotten started. Suddenly your goal turns into a nightmare. Now you start using inner voice messages like "I'll never get this done." Or, "if only I had enough time to complete the assignment." Or, "Maybe I can start tomorrow." As the pressure increases to get the project completed, you start using the negative Bummer words as excuses. And, if you answered the two key **REALITY TIME QUESTIONS**, you would have to say "no" that you had not given your best effort. What to do?

CHANGE your inner voice messages and get busy. You can still reach your goal, but this measurement-check suggests that you need to make some changes to get there. Take a couple of minutes to write down a plan for completing the project on time and getting it done correctly. Eliminate the Bummer words. Use the positive "YES! Count On Me" words and start working your plan. Yes, it will be a little more difficult with only three days left, but you can do it. Take positive action to reach your goal.

TAKING RESPONSIBILITY: You can measure your progress toward reaching your goals by taking more responsibility. Do you ever get tired of hearing "do this," "do that" and "don't do that?" It's maddening sometimes, isn't it? But, have you ever stopped to think about why your parents, teachers and other adults are always "after you?" Is it possible they are trying to help you? How can that be?

YOU will find that in reality, there are very few people who are looking for ways to specifically "nag you." More often they are trying to teach you important lessons that will help you later in your life. How does taking the trash out, studying for a test or doing homework help you learn about life? It's called responsibility.

TAKING responsibility is doing something without being asked because you know it needs to get done. As you get older, you will be asked to take on more and more responsibility, and it is important to learn how to do it. If you know you have to take out the trash, practice your piano lesson or do your homework and you don't – you are not taking responsibility. Don't wait to be asked over and over again. See what has to be done, or how you can help someone else, and do it.

Measure Your Progress 41

**ONE** of the ways to tell you are growing up is when you start to take responsibility for yourself without being asked fifteen times. Want to stop "people hassling you all the time?" That's easy - show them you are growing up by remembering to do something without being asked over and over again.

**COMPLETING** Your Action Steps: The fourth way to measure the progress toward reaching your goals is with the Action Steps. Remember that Action Steps are like the rungs of a ladder with the goal at the top. You develop a specific plan for reaching your goal by writing down the goal, making a list of specific Action Steps and setting a Target Date. Acting on your plan, (the Action Steps), will move you toward reaching your goal.

**COMPLETING** each of the Action Steps is an excellent way to measure your progress toward reaching your goal. Let's say your goal is to earn $100 to buy a new bike. You may decide that your Action Steps will include finding three neighbors lawns to mow per week, putting an ad in the paper for babysitting jobs and washing the family car each week. You have set a Target Date to complete your goal to earn $100 by July 15th. By the end of June, if you have not put the ad in the paper and are mowing only one neighbor's lawn, you are going to have problems reaching your goal. As you complete your Action Steps, you will be able to check your progress toward reaching your goal.

**HELPING OTHERS:** How often are you *helping others?* In today's world there are plenty of people who belong to the "it's all about me" club. Many people mistakenly believe it's a "me, me, me" world and stay very focused on themselves. These people miss a really important part of life - helping others.

**IT** is important for you to help others. *Successful* people set goals. *Successful* people measure their progress toward reaching those goals. *Successful* people enjoy their *success*, they have many friends, they have a good self-image and they know the importance of helping others. Help others for a richer, fuller life.

Let's review the important components to measuring your progress.

1. Make your reality time count. Be sincere about your efforts toward reaching your goals.

2. Each time you complete one of your Action Steps you are getting closer to your goal.

3. Always have a positive mental attitude.

4. Take responsibility for yourself and your actions.

5. Enjoy life to it's fullest by helping others.

# Key Vocabulary Words

Fill in the missing words in each sentence with the correct word from the right hand column.

**Responsibility**   **Reality**
**Helping others**   **Self-Image**
**Positive**

1. I choose to have my _____ - _____ be positive.
2. It is my _____ to make my self-image positive.
3. _____ time is a chance for me to "look in the mirror" and measure how I am progressing toward my goal.
4. It is important for me to have a _____ mental attitude.
5. If you are _____ you have less time to think only of yourself.

Anita was a good student and wanted to "fit in" with the other students at her new school. Unfortunately, she had a negative self-image. She thought the other kids would not like her as much because she wasn't "like they were." Because she didn't feel good about herself, she used a lot of "Bummer Words" in her inner voice messages on the way to school.

Some of her negative inner voice messages included: "I won't be able to get them to like me," "I can't," "I'm afraid," "I've never done that before" and "If only I could." These negative thoughts were holding Anita back from reaching her goal of "fitting in" at the new school. She was letting her fears stop her from trying.

Anita realized that she needed to take some responsibility for not fitting in. During her reality time, she realized that she needed to make some changes. In those quiet moments she had to be honest with herself that she was not giving a 100% effort to meet new kids and that she was spending too much time thinking negatively.

She talked to a school counselor who told her that she was a really neat person that the other kids would like. The counselor reminded Anita that she was good at computers, a good student and that she was probably one of the best girl's soccer players in the school. Anita realized that the counselor was right and that she had a lot going for herself. When she thought about it, she realized that she was too focused on the negative thoughts. Further, she realized that she should have been thinking about all the positive things she had going for her, like being good at computers and soccer.

Anita decided to take the responsibility to change her self-image. She decided on several Action Steps. First, she decided to minimize the Bummer Words. Each day she kept a count of the negative words she used. Anita made a point to use at least one less "Bummer Word" each day. Also, she replaced them with positive up-beat "I'll make it happen" words *yes, I will,* and *I can.*

Her second Action Step was to meet at least one new person at school a day. Once she started to meet more kids she found several students who shared her interest in computers. She also learned that the kids liked her a lot more than she thought they did.

Third, Anita realized that one of the best ways to improve her self-image was by helping others. If she was helping others, Anita realized she would be too busy to worry about whether she was fitting in. Anita's fourth Action Step was to join one of the school organizations. She chose the drama club.

After a couple of weeks Anita had met a lot of new students` and was helping the Drama Club build a new background for their school play. She was so busy she forgot about trying to fit in. Anita reached her goal of fitting in because she took the responsibility to set a goal and develop a specific plan with Action Steps. Before long Anita was accepted at school and felt good about herself again.

**1.** What Action Steps did Anita create to reach her goal of "fitting in?"

1. _____
2. _____
3. _____
4. _____

**2.** This may shock you, but your teachers have goals for what they want to teach you. These goals are called lesson plans. Teachers write lesson plans for a day, a week or a month. How do you think your teachers can measure progress toward reaching their goals for your class? (Hint! Tests are one example).

1. _____
2. _____
3. _____
4. _____

**3.** As a class exercise, count the number of times in the week that the entire class uses the words "yes", "I can" and "I will." On the blackboard write your class's goal for the week - how many times the entire class says "yes," "I can" and "I will."

Each day track your class's progress toward reaching the goal. On your Target Date, did you reach your goal? What lessons did you learn from this exercise?

1. _____
2. _____
3. _____
4. _____

**4.** "Don't be afraid to fail. Experience is just mistakes you won't make again."

*Joe Garagiola*

What did Joe Garagiola mean? Can you give an example to illustrate this idea? What might make someone afraid to fail? What Action Steps could a person take to overcome fear?

_____
_____
_____
_____

**1.** Earlier we discussed the importance of "reality time" and being sincere with yourself when answering two questions:

1) Am I giving my best effort to today's activities?

2) Am I making progress toward reaching my goal(s)?

Considering your efforts in class today, how do you answer these questions?

_____
_____
_____
_____

**2.** "Do something for somebody everyday for which you do not get paid."

*Albert Schweitzer*

Think about the above quote. Do you agree with this quote? Why do you think this is a good idea? Explain.

_____
_____
_____
_____

**3.** With your parents or caregivers, develop a plan to help someone (or an organization) for one week.

★ Name the person or organization you will help:

_____

★ Your goal - what will you and your parents/caregivers do to help them?:

_____

★ What will your Action Steps be?:

1. _____
2. _____
3. _____
4. _____

★ Target Date to complete goal. _____

**DREAM + Action Steps + TARGET DATE = Goal**

This is *your* life, *your* goals and *your success*.
You are a **Winner!**

*I make a $100,000 a year*

Measure Your Progress

# Chapter 6: Meeting the Challenge

**What To Expect**
* Potential roadblocks to success.
* Minimize excuses.
* Changing roadblocks into minor setbacks.

## Words to Remember
Fear of failure
Peer pressure
Determination

## Preview

WE have learned that goal setting is a very important part of being *success*ful and, we know that most people want to be *success*ful. So why aren't more people setting goals?

CERTAINLY one of the reasons is that many people do not know how to set and achieve goals (this is why this workbook is so valuable). Another reason is that there are roadblocks or challenges to success. In this chapter we will learn about potential roadblocks and how to minimize or eliminate them.

FOUR major challenges or potential roadblocks are:

1. Fear of failure
2. Lack of determination
3. Peer pressure
4. Excuses, excuses.

★ THE *fear of failure* is a strong negative influence. It means you fear what others might think or say about you. In many cases, this fear of failure roadblock can stop a person from trying new things. They become afraid to try something because they might make a mistake.

FOR example: a student was asked to do a math problem on the blackboard. He was afraid he would-

48  Goal Setting for Students

n't do it correctly and that the other students might make fun of him. So he did not try. His fear of failure defeated him before he even tried. Have you ever had fear of failure effect you? If you have had a case of "fear of failure" – you're not alone. Almost everyone does sometimes in their life.

THERE is a cure for fear of failure. Yes, you guessed it – **GOAL SETTING**. Certainly, there are risks in setting a goal and, it is true, you may not reach the goal. But, if you let fear of failure set in, you won't even try. Set your goal and, if for some reason you don't reach it, learn from the experience. Don't let *fear of failure* stop you from trying new things. Meet the challenge! Don't let *fear of failure* conquer you!

★ANOTHER potential roadblock to your *success* is lack of determination. *Determination* is having the guts not to quit when the going gets tough. Many people don't have it. They try something once and because they did not do it well, they don't try it again. Then they make excuses. When you set a goal, and have the determination to complete it, setbacks become a problem to overcome rather than a stopping point. When you are determined or strong-minded about reaching your goals, you will figure out ways to overcome challenges. Remember we talked earlier about the importance of having someone whom you trust and who will help you? This person, a mentor, can be a valuable resource in helping you overcome challenges. Be determined not to quit when you meet a challenge on your path to *success*. Have the courage to ask for help when you need it.

WHEN you were learning to ride your two-wheeled bicycle for the first time, did you fall and scrape your knees a couple of times? Did you get back on the bike and try again? Then, after enough practice, you rode your bike with no problem. In fact, now you can probably ride without having your hands on the handlebars.

THAT'S determination! You wanted to ride your bike, and the falls were only minor setbacks. You were focused on your goal and willing to keep trying until you learned how to do it. Determination is the lesson we learned when we started to ride our first bicycle. **Your determination to keep trying will help you reach new and higher goals.**

★ **PEER PRESSURE** can be very difficult. It is one of the roadblocks people encounter on the road to setting and completing their goals. Other kids in your age group might be saying it's cool to smoke, not to do your homework, to stay out late or to skip practice. **Peer pressure is doing what the group wants you to do even if you don't want to.** You probably already know exactly what we mean by peer pressure. Ever say to your parents "But Mom, everyone is doing it?"

HERE'S an example of **peer pressure**: You set a goal to learn how to play the piano. You take lessons and the teacher says that you should practice thirty minutes per day. You start to practice every day and you want to continue to improve. You know that to improve will mean practicing when you would rather be doing something else. Some of the kids from school are going to the mall and they want you to join them. You say yes and stop practicing the piano. Peer pressure has sidetracked you from reaching your goal.

IF this was a game and we were keeping score, it would be one point for the peer pressure group and no points for you. **Funny thing, the peer group is out scoring you in your game of life. There will always be peer pressure. It is your responsibility to stay focused on your goals even when you have peer pressure.**

★ **EXCUSES, excuses, excuses! The world is full of people who make excuses.** Excuses are roadblocks. Do you know people who make excuses for not handing in their homework on time or for not doing well in a class? Excuses shift the blame to someone or something else. For example, "I would have handed in my homework, but the dog ate it." Or, Miranda always gets good grades because she is the teacher's pet, when really she works harder than you do to get the good grades. Don't let excuses be a roadblock to your *success*.

FAST forward several years and you are now working at a job that pays you $30,000 per year. Your boss comes in and says he needs your report on his desk in the morning. Are you going to work the next day and tell him "my dog ate my report?" Do you think you will be employed long? To make your goals become a reality it is very important to eliminate excuses.

USE your imagination, your desire and your determination to succeed. Eliminate or minimize roadblocks. Goal setting with Action Steps can change roadblocks into minor setbacks.

Let's review the important components of meeting your challenges.

**1.** Conquer your *fear of failure*. Be willing to risk making a mistake. Learn valuable lessons from them.

**2.** Have the guts to keep going toward your goals even when the going gets tough.

**3.** Don't let peer pressure side track you from reaching your goals.

**4.** Eliminate excuses.

# Key Vocabulary Words

Fill in the missing words in each sentence with the correct word below.

| | |
|---|---|
| **Excuses** | **Peer pressure** |
| **Fear of failure** | **Determination** |
| **Setback** | **Roadblocks** |
| **Goal setting** | |

1. A cure for fear of failure is _____.

2. In reaching for your goals there will be _____, but don't let them stop you.

3. _____ is when you try and try again to reach your goal without giving up or making excuses.

4. Don't let _____ become an excuse for not reaching your goal.

5. _____ can cause you to quit on your goal before you succeed. (Don't let that happen to you.)

6. _____ means you fear what others might think or say about you.

7. The world is full of people who make _____.

Hector is a good kid, gets good grades, is about average in sports and is popular with the other kids in the neighborhood. But Hector did not feel good about himself. Hector is a kid that has a lot of positive things going for him but that is not how he sees himself. He sees himself differently than how others see him. He has a low self-image. Because of it, he does not try new things. In fact, Hector has a case of fear of failure.

Hector started to hang around a different crowd at school. Hector's new group was more interested in "acting the fool", not doing their homework, and giving a hard time to students who were going to school to learn. Because of *peer pressure* from his new group, Hector soon started to act like they did. He was acquiring their bad habits. Hector went along with them because he was afraid of what the group might think or say about him if he didn't.

Mary was in Hector's grade, and even at that age, she knew she wanted to go to college to become a veterinarian. She knew she would have to study hard to get into college. Mary had the *determination* to put in the extra effort to reach her goal. Some of her Action Steps included listening to the teacher in class, asking good questions, doing all of her homework, studying for the tests and even included doing extra credit projects.

Many of the things Mary was doing and learning were new to her. Like everyone else, she was afraid she would make a mistake and embarrass herself in class. But her determination to reach her goal to be an animal doctor gave her the courage to learn valuable lessons from those mistakes. She would not let her fear of failure become a roadblock to her success.

One day Mary was walking home from school and went past Hector and his new group. They started to call her "teacher's pet" and other names. They made fun of Mary because she was getting good grades. Hector wasn't 100% sure he wanted to hassle Mary, but because of peer pressure he went along with the group. Soon Hector realized that Mary was really hurt by what they were saying. He told the group to stop. Hector realized that it wasn't as cool as he thought to "act the fool."

Hector figured out that joining this new group was an excuse for not taking some responsibility. He began to recognize that he needed to change his self-image. He knew that he needed to try new things - even if he made a mistake. Hector was now determined to change his self-image. He apologized to Mary for hurting her feelings. Hector took control of his life, eliminated his roadblocks and began to set goals for himself. Today he is a happy, well-adjusted kid. He doesn't make excuses. Hector takes responsibility for his own actions.

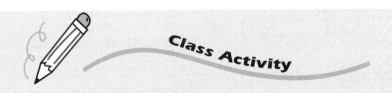

**1.** What goals do you think the members of Hector's new group have?

**2.** How should Mary handle the hateful words Hector's group was calling her?

**3.** In this chapter we learned that there are challenges that can hold you back from reaching our goals. These challenges include: a) fear of failure, b) peer pressure, c) a lack of determination and d) excuses. Which of these challenges do you think hold most people back from reaching their goals? Explain.

**4.** Let's say you are the teacher of this class. It is your responsibility to teach your classmates. From your new point of view -the teacher's - what challenges do you think are keeping your students from being successful?

**5.** "All glory comes from daring to begin."

*Eugene Ware*

What does Eugene Ware mean? Do you agree? How could you put this idea into practice?

## Home Activity

**1.** Talk with your parents about the "fear of failure." Do they know anyone whose life was damaged by it? Have they ever experience it? How do they think someone can overcome their fear of failure?

**2.** "I've missed more than 9000 shots in my career. Twenty-six times I've been trusted to take the game winning shot and missed. I've failed over and over and over again in life. And, that is why I succeed."  *Michael Jordan*

How can it be true that missing 9,000 shots helped Michael Jordon succeed? How is Michael's life an example of determination? How does determination work off the basketball court – in school?

_____
_____
_____
_____

**3.** Can you think of examples of peer pressure that you have experienced?

_____
_____
_____
_____

**4.** Find an example in a magazine or book where a person's determination gave them the courage to reach their goal. Briefly write what you learned form the article.

_____
_____
_____
_____

# CHAPTER 7: How to get Started

## What To Expect
★ Ten points to remember.
★ Where do I start.
★ Thank you – Ben Franklin.
★ Education Contract.

**Words to Remember**

"Education is your window to the world."
John Bishop

## Preview

**GOAL SETTING** will change your life and give you a sense of direction. The principles are relatively easy to learn, but it will take effort on your part to change your habits and include goal setting as a regular part of your future. Here are some hints to help you get started:

1. Find the answers to these four questions:
   * What do I want?   * When do I want it?
   * Why do I want it?  * How will I get it?

2. Start by setting and achieving smaller, reachable goals. Build on your successes.

3. Write your Goals, Action Steps, and Target Date on a piece of paper. Carry your written goals in your pocket and read them everyday.

4. Develop an "I'll Make It Happen" attitude.

5. Eliminate excuses and take action toward reaching your goals.

6. Don't be afraid to ask for help.

7. Answer these questions positively each day.
   a. Am I giving my best effort to today's activities?
   b. Am I making progress toward reaching my goals?

8. Use positive words – I will, yes and I can.

9. Remember to help others.

10. If you have reached your goal, congratulate yourself for a job well done. If you missed the goal, explore the reasons why.

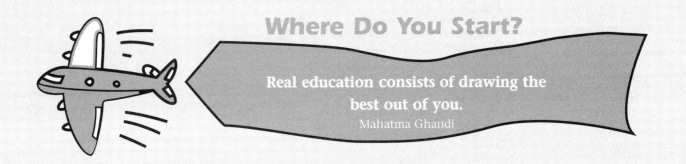

# Where Do You Start?

*Real education consists of drawing the best out of you.*
Mahatma Ghandi

**The best place for you to start using Goal Setting for Students** techniques is right here – right now. Your schooling is extremely important to your future and, the teacher giving you instruction on goal setting can help you. But, you have to help them also.

**REMEMBER** what we said about responsibility? Taking *responsibility* is doing something without being asked because you know it needs to get done. Take responsibility for *your* education. Yes, that will mean doing your homework, checking it before you hand it in, reviewing the subject before tests, listening in class and taking part in the class discussions. Taking responsibility means not making excuses for a lack of effort on your part. Your ability to take responsibility for your education now will have major impact on your future.

**START** by taking one subject and challenge yourself by setting a "stretch" goal to improve in that subject. Make the goal realistic and achievable, but make it one where you have to stretch your abilities. Write the goal down and include your Action Steps and target date. If you achieve your goal - reward yourself and then set another goal. Start to make goal setting a habit in your life.

**WHAT** happens if *you* don't reach your goal? First, you should know that you will not make 100% of your goals – nobody does. If you miss the goal then use it as a learning tool. Did you set the goal too high? Was there a lack of effort? What could you have done differently to give yourself a better chance for *success*? Did you make a lot of excuses? Did you write your goal down and read it everyday? What can you learn from the experience? After you have learned from this lesson, set another goal and try again.

**ON** the next page you will be asked to write down what you did during a couple of days. This is a chance for you to look at how you are spending your time. A friend of mine once said that each day we wake up with 24 "gold coins," one for each hour of the day. During the day you have to spend your "gold coins" for eating, sleeping, school, seeing friends, etc. How did you use all of your "gold coins" for the day? Do you have a couple "coins" at the end of the day to spend doing something that is important for your future? For two days, write down how you spent your time during the day.

*A journey starts with a single step.*
Chinese Proverb

**How to get Started**

# My Day

| | EXAMPLE | | Day # 1 | | Day # 2 |
|---|---|---|---|---|---|
| 6:30 | Wake up | 6:30 | | 6:30 | |
| 7:00 | Breakfast | 7:00 | | 7:00 | |
| 7:30 | Bus to school | 7:30 | | 7:30 | |
| 8:00 | School | 8:00 | | 8:00 | |
| 8:30 | School | 8:30 | | 8:30 | |
| 9:00 | School | 9:00 | | 9:00 | |
| 9:30 | School | 9:30 | | 9:30 | |
| 10:00 | School | 10:00 | | 10:00 | |
| 10:30 | School | 10:30 | | 10:30 | |
| 11:00 | School | 11:00 | | 11:00 | |
| 11:30 | School | 11:30 | | 11:30 | |
| Noon | Lunch | Noon | | Noon | |
| 12:30 | School | 12:30 | | 12:30 | |
| 1:00 | School | 1:00 | | 1:00 | |
| 1:30 | School | 1:30 | | 1:30 | |
| 2:00 | School | 2:00 | | 2:00 | |
| 2:30 | School | 2:30 | | 2:30 | |
| 3:00 | Bus home | 3:00 | | 3:00 | |
| 3:30 | Time with friends | 3:30 | | 3:30 | |
| 4:00 | Time with friends | 4:00 | | 4:00 | |
| 4:30 | Time with friends | 4:30 | | 4:30 | |
| 5:00 | Watch TV | 5:00 | | 5:00 | |
| 5:30 | Watch TV | 5:30 | | 5:30 | |
| 6:00 | Watch TV | 6:00 | | 6:00 | |
| 6:30 | Dinner | 6:30 | | 6:30 | |
| 7:00 | Homework | 7:00 | | 7:00 | |
| 7:30 | Homework | 7:30 | | 7:30 | |
| 8:00 | Homework | 8:00 | | 8:00 | |
| 8:30 | Watch TV | 8:30 | | 8:30 | |
| 9:00 | Watch TV | 9:00 | | 9:00 | |
| 9:30 | Bedtime | 9:30 | | 9:30 | |

**Suggested additional topics**: video games, reading, hobbies, after school activities, time on the computer, chores at home, part-time job, etc. **Review** your results after the second day. What did you learn? Did you use your time wisely? Can you find a way to use your time better in the future?

# My Day

My goal for the next three days is: _____

| | Day # 1 | | Day # 2 | | Day # 3 |
|---|---|---|---|---|---|
| 6:30 | | :30 | | 6:30 | |
| 7:00 | | 7:00 | | 7:00 | |
| 7:30 | | 7:30 | | 7:30 | |
| 8:00 | | 8:00 | | 8:00 | |
| 8:30 | | 8:30 | | 8:30 | |
| 9:00 | | 9:00 | | 9:00 | |
| 9:30 | | 9:30 | | 9:30 | |
| 10:00 | | 10:00 | | 10:00 | |
| 10:30 | | 10:30 | | 10:30 | |
| 11:00 | | 11:00 | | 11:00 | |
| 11:30 | | 11:30 | | 11:30 | |
| Noon | | Noon | | Noon | |
| 12:30 | | 12:30 | | 12:30 | |
| 1:00 | | 1:00 | | 1:00 | |
| 1:30 | | 1:30 | | 1:30 | |
| 2:00 | | 2:00 | | 2:00 | |
| 2:30 | | 2:30 | | 2:30 | |
| 3:00 | | 3:00 | | 3:00 | |
| 3:30 | | 3:30 | | 3:30 | |
| 4:00 | | 4:00 | | 4:00 | |
| 4:30 | | 4:30 | | 4:30 | |
| 5:00 | | 5:00 | | 5:00 | |
| 5:30 | | 5:30 | | 5:30 | |
| 6:00 | | 6:00 | | 6:00 | |
| 6:30 | | 6:30 | | 6:30 | |
| 7:00 | | 7:00 | | 7:00 | |
| 7:30 | | 7:30 | | 7:30 | |
| 8:00 | | 8:00 | | 8:00 | |
| 8:30 | | 8:30 | | 8:30 | |
| 9:00 | | 9:00 | | 9:00 | |
| 9:30 | | 9:30 | | 9:30 | |

How many minutes did you spend trying to reach your goal? _____ minutes

Your personal effort toward reaching your goal was: 100%_____ 75% _____ 50%_____

What did you learn? Did you use your time wisely? How can you give more effort toward reaching your goals during the next three days?

## Thank you - Ben Franklin!

Most of us know Ben Franklin for his role in United States history. He was a printer, author, inventor, our U.S. Ambassador to France and a signer of the Declaration of Independence. However, you many not know that he used goals to fulfill and enhance is life.

Ben Franklin believed in character development. He felt that an exemplary person would excel in the 13 character traits listed below. Mr. Franklin had a plan for a successful life. It was simple and creative. He set a goal to improve one characteristic per week. During that week, he focused on that specific characteristic.

The next week he would work on another character trait with equal determination. Week after week he focused on one area to improve. When he finished with all 13 self-improvement characteristics, he started over again. He had a goal, action steps, and timetable. He worked his plan for over 50 years – one week and one characteristic at a time.

Below are the character traits Ben Franklin worked on to improve his chances for success.

| CHARACTER TRAIT | DESCRIPTION |
| --- | --- |
| Self-control | Be determined and disciplined in your efforts. |
| Silence | Listen better in all discussions. |
| Order | Don't agonize – organize. |
| Determination | Promise to put your best effort into today's activities. |
| Thrift | Watch how you spend your money and your time. |
| Effectiveness | Work hard – work smart. |
| Fairness | Treat others the way you want to be treated. |
| Moderation | Avoid extremes. |
| Cleanliness | Have clean mind, body and habits. |
| Tranquility | Take time to slow down and "smell the roses." |
| Charity | Help others. |
| Humility | Keep your ego in check. |
| Sincerity | Be honest with yourself and others. |

60  Goal Setting for Students

### Are you up to a challenge?

Start by choosing four of Ben Franklin's characteristics. Set a goal to work to improve on these four traits in the next month. Focus on one of the traits for a week. Then, move to another characteristic on your list for the next week. At the end of each week, evaluate how you did with your goal, action steps and timetable to improve in that specific area.

At the end of the month, you can either start over again with the first area you choice to improve or add more characteristics to your list. Be determined and focused on the trait you are working on for the week. Notice how often during the week you have an opportunity to positively improve.

# MY EDUCATION CONTRACT

I understand that I must take a pro-active approach to my education. I realize my teacher(s) and my parent/caregivers are there to help me succeed. In taking responsibility for my education, I will:

* Listen better in class.
* Take better classroom notes.
* Participate more in the classroom discussions.
* Look over the chapter before it is discussed in class.
* Read the chapter and review my notes from class before doing my homework.
* Ask the teacher questions if I did not understand the material.
* Write down the homework assignments correctly.
* Three days before a test, spend some extra time studying on that subject.
* The night before the test ask someone to help me study.
* Do projects for extra credit.
* Change my seating assignment in class, if necessary.
* Hand in my homework on time.
* Take a few moments to check my homework before handing it in.

I agree to inform my teacher or my parents/caregivers when I am having a difficult time with my commitment to this contract.

_____  _____
(STUDENT)                                    (DATE)

_____  _____
(TEACHER)                                    (DATE)

_____  _____
(PARENT/CAREGIVER)                    (DATE)

# Chapter 8 Summary

**What To Expect**

★ Two key questions to ask each day.
1. Am I giving my best effort to today's activities?
2. Am I making progress toward reaching my goal(s)?

**Words to Remember**

"Happiness depends upon ourselves."

Aristotle

## Preview

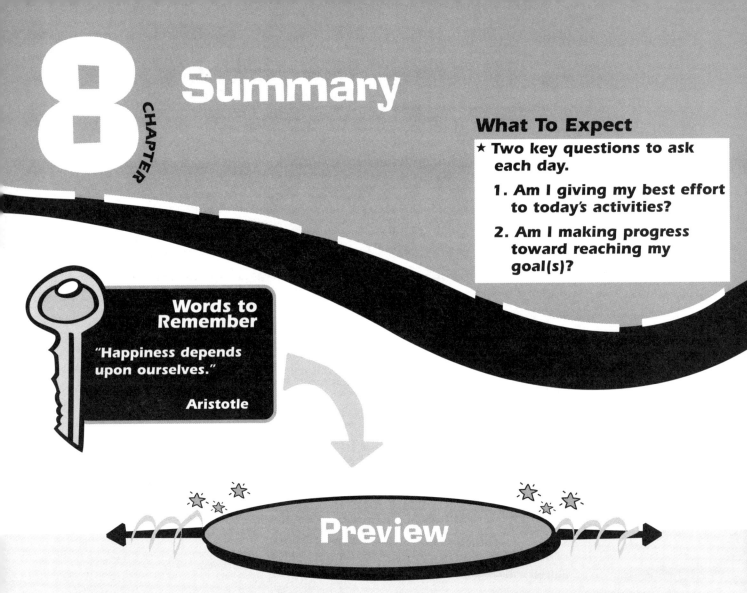

IN this program we covered material about *success* and the importance of goal setting. You learned that *success* does not have to mean that you are the richest, the smartest, the prettiest or the most famous. *Success*ful people can be truck drivers, farmers, athletes, schoolteachers, nurses and housewives. *Success* is what you make it. *Success* is being as good as you can be.

**SUCCESS** is putting your best effort toward reaching your goals. *Success* is knowing that in your quiet moments of "reality time" you aren't making excuses for falling short of your goals. *Success* is knowing that you tried your very best – that you had the desire and determination to succeed. *Success* is having a "*can do*" and "*will do*" attitude and begins with your belief in yourself and your abilities. Also, *success* is knowing that at times you may not reach your goal. When that happens, and it will, you have the self-confidence and determination to learn from those disappointments.

**WITH** *success* comes responsibility. You are responsible for your *success*. It is important to have dreams. To be *success*ful you have to turn your dreams into goals. Write your goals on a piece of paper and develop a plan. Your plan must include *Action Steps* and a Target Date for completion. Remember the story about the archer pointing an arrow at a target. He may want to hit the target, but until he takes action – shooting the arrow – he is only dreaming. Make sure you take action toward your goals – your target.

**RESPONSIBILITY means that you are in charge of "making it happen" in your life.** You are at the controls of your inner voice – just you. It is your responsibility to control that inner voice. Remember those "bummer words" you want to eliminate? They are – maybe, if, can't, won't, no and never. Minimize the "bummer words." They are negative and will hold you back from reaching your full potential. Substitute positive upbeat words. Use words like: *"Yes," "I can" and "I will."*

GEORGE Washington Carver, a famous scientist, once said: "99% of failures come from people who practice the habit of making excuses." As you get older you will see how very true these words are. Far too many people hide from their fears with excuses. Don't make excuses. Helen Keller was blind and deaf. She could have easily made excuses. Instead she got busy. She became famous for writing several books including one that was made into a movie about her life. She did not let her fears become excuses.

CONQUER YOUR FEARS! You will find that most of your fears will be between your ears. Your mind can paint negative or positive pictures. Your mind can make you fearful or it can make you strong. Too many people are afraid to make a mistake so they don't try new and exciting things. Don't let your fears hold you back from doing the things you want in life. Setting goals and creating actions steps will let you tackle your fears in small steps until you reach your goal. After reaching your goal, you can look back at your fear. Then, you will realize that your fear wasn't as large as you first thought. Most importantly, you will feel good about overcoming the challenge--your fear—and completing your goal.

REMEMBER that it is important to help others. You are not alone. Many people have helped you to get to this point in your life. Be willing to give a helping hand to someone who may need it. If your goals and your definition of *success* only include you, you may live a very lonely life. Have goals to meet someone new each week, to do volunteer work and to simply help around the house without being asked.

Let's review the important components to the **Goal Setting for Students**™ program.

1. *Success* is putting your best effort toward reaching your goals.
2. With *success* comes responsibility.
3. Be positive about yourself and honest about your efforts.
4. Answer these questions positively each day.
    a. Am I giving my best effort to today's activities?
    b. Am I making progress toward reaching my goals?
5. Conquer your fears. You will find most of them will be between your ears.
6. Put your dreams into action.
7. Help others.

We have all heard about Abraham Lincoln. You know that he was one of our most famous Presidents and that he was in office during the Civil War more than 100 years ago. In his effort to become the President, he faced many setbacks. Those setbacks would have stopped most people before they reached the goal, but not Mr. Lincoln. He remained determined to reach his goal. Below are some of the challenges President Lincoln overcame:

★ He had two businesses that went bankrupt.
★ He ran for public office eight times and lost each time.
★ He tried to be elected to Congress four times and failed each time.
★ He lost the election for Vice President.

We remember him as a great President. Now you know that this famous person, our 16th President, had a great many obstacles to overcome to reach his goal and be successful. He was determined to keep trying to reach his goal.

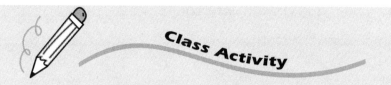

**1.** Discuss two important things you learned from Abraham Lincoln's life. Do your classmates agree with your views? Explore with them areas where they might disagree.

1. _____
2. _____

**2.** "People never plan to be failures; they simply fail to plan to be successful."

*William Ward*

What does this quote mean to you? Explain.

_____
_____
_____
_____

## Home Activity

**1.** Share the story about Abe Lincoln with your parents. Discuss with them what you learned from the story.

**2.** "A ship in a safe harbor is safe, but that is not what a ship was built for."

*William Shedd*

Discuss with your parents/caregivers what this quote means to you.

### DREAM + ACTION STEPS + TARGET DATE = GOAL

**This is your life, your goals, and your success.**
**You are a Winner!**

# NOTES

# ACKNOWLEDGEMENTS

**THERE** are a great many people to thank for nurturing this project to fruition. Their guidance, encouragement and collective wisdom helped to make the Goal Setting for Students™ program a reality. Hopefully, I will not leave anyone out, but several people deserve special recognition for their efforts.

**FIRST** and foremost, I dedicate this book to my wife, Carole Hale-Bishop, and granddaughter, Miranda Bishop. They deserve very special credit for being contributors, sounding boards, proof readers and critics. Each contributed far more than they know.

**STEPHEN JOHNSON** has been a source of solid business knowledge and judgment which has been extremely helpful in bringing the program to market. Jim Buford, President of the St. Louis Urban League, has a sincere understanding of the needs of inner city students and he has helped me immeasurably. Rev. Jerry Paul and George Oehlert have been particularly helpful in giving me their guidance and enthusiasm for life. Importantly, each of these four men has a very special gift for helping others to reach their full potential.

**THREE** people have made special contributions to the program. Susan Spence, a mother of four, is truly dedicated to the principles of goal setting and personal responsibility. Her enthusiasm for the project is unmatched. With her educational background, she has been a source of direction and inspiration. Dr. Jane Fryar has consistently given me wise counsel on creating a curriculum to maximize the positive messages of the text. Tamara Clerkley is the finest graphic artist I have ever worked with. She took our program content and made it "student friendly." Her workbook cover graphics, promotional brochure and website make the **Goal Setting for Students**™ message "jump off the page."

**IN** addition, several other teachers, administrators, parents and friends read some of the earlier versions and gave valuable input on how to enhance the goal setting message to students. Two people who were particularly helpful are Drs. Melinda Bier and Stephen Sherblom. Both have a great ability to get to the heart of the issue and make points clear to the reader.